The Luckless Age

The Luckless Age

POEMS

Steve Kistulentz

RED HEN PRESS | PASADENA, CA

The Luckless Age
Copyright © 2011 by Steve Kistulentz
All rights reserved

Book layout by Leila Benoun
Book design by Mark E. Cull

Library of Congress Cataloging-in-Publication Data
Kistulentz, Steve.
The luckless age / Steve Kistulentz. —1st ed.
    p. cm.
Poems.
ISBN 978-1-59709-494-8
I. Title.
PS3611.I875L83 2011
811'.6—dc22
                    2010041520

The California Arts Council, the Los Angeles County Arts Commission, the National Endowment for the Arts, and Department of Cultural Affairs City of Los Angeles partially support Red Hen Press.

First Edition
Published by Red Hen Press
www.redhen.org

Acknowledgements

I wish to thank the editors of the following journals and anthologies where these poems appeared, some in slightly different form: *No Tell Motel*: "The David Lee Roth Fuck Poem with Language Taken from *Van Halen I, 1984*, and the First Letter of the Apostle Paul to the Church at Corinth," "Wonderamaland," "Hot Child in the City," "Fuck Poem with Language Borrowed from *Brothers Karamazov*," and "Fuck Poem with Language Borrowed from the Gospel According to Saint Mark"; *Best New Poets 2008*, edited by Mark Strand, series editor Jeb Livingood: "The David Lee Roth Fuck Poem . . ."; *Drunken Boat*: "The Sinatra Villanelle"; *Ava Gardner: Touches of Venus*, editor Gil Gigliotti: "The Sinatra Villanelle"; *Quarterly West*: "The Picture of Hank Williams, Sr., Taken by My Grandfather in Germany" and "Elegy for the Bay City Rollers"; *Paterson Literary Review*: "The End of the Affair as Foretold in Language from the Revelation of Saint John the Divine" (under the title "Divination"); *New England Review*: "The Bourbon Myths" and "Fixing"; *Helen Burns Poetry Anthology: New Voices from the Academy of American Poets' University and College Prizes*, edited by Mark Doty: "Bargain"; *Barrelhouse*: "Bargain"; *Caesura*: ". . . but the Little Girls Understand"; *LaFovea*: "Roaratorio"; *Black Warrior Review*: "Playing the Lead"; *Vox*: "Changeling"; *Southeast Review*: "Abyssinia."

"The City Bleeds (Parts I and II)" and "Bargain" were awarded the 2007 John Mackay Shaw Academy of American Poets Prize, judged by Campbell McGrath. "The Skipper Talks to His Therapist" was awarded the 2006 John Mackay Shaw Academy of American Poets Prize, judged by Denise Duhamel.

A number of poems recognize their inspiration colloquially, but where they do not, I wish to acknowledge the following artists whose work influenced individual poems: Iggy Pop, Lou Reed, Bauhaus, Tommy Keene, Marginal Man, Government

Issue, The U.K. Subs, Mike Doughty and Soul Coughing, John Doe and X, John Lennon, The Knack, Nick Gilder, Bo Diddley, Pat Travers, and The Who. Part I of "The Luckless Age" begins with a paraphrase of a line from Czeslaw Milosz's poem "Preparation." Part II takes its title from a song by Tommy Keene. "Roaratorio" takes some vocabulary from Julio Cortazar's *Hopscotch*. "Fuck Poem with Language Borrowed from the Gospel According to Saint Mark" takes its conclusion from the story of the lunatic, found in Chapter 5. The line "Los Angeles beckons the teenagers to come to her on buses," which appears in the poems "Wild Gift" and "Hot Child in the City," is taken from the Soul Coughing song "Screenwriter's Blues." "Fuck Poem with Language Borrowed from *Brothers Karamazov*" was inspired by the short film *Surviving Desire*, directed by Hal Hartley.

I am indebted to Nick Flynn for picking this book out of many worthy manuscripts. The writing of this book was greatly aided by support from the University of Iowa, The Edward and Marie C. Kingsbury Award from the Florida State University College of Arts and Sciences, and the Virginia Center for the Creative Arts. Thank you all.

For guidance—editorial and otherwise—I thank my many gifted teachers, especially: John Conlee, Peter Wiggins, David Clay Jenkins, Natasha Sajé, Glenn Moomau, Alan Cheuse, George Garrett, Frank Conroy, Chris Offutt, Jennifer Vanderbes, Ethan Canin, Thisbe Nissen, Elizabeth McCracken, Edward Carey, Mark Winegardner, Robert Olen Butler, Erin Belieu, David Kirby, and Julianna Baggott.

For encouragement, friendship, editorial advice, I'm grateful to Mary Biddinger, Tom Bligh, Barbara Hamby, Allison Joseph, Erika Meitner, Martha

Silano, Margot Schilpp, Eric Lee, Daniel Khalastchi, Ian Stansel, Sarah Strickley, David Philip Mullins, Kurt Gutjahr, Michael Garriga, Frank Giampietro; Dave Housley, Mike Ingram, Dan Brady, Matt Kirkpatrick, Tom McAlister and all of team Barrelhouse. Lee Klein. Damon Sauve. C. Dale Young. Judith Hall. Reb Livingston. Chip Theodore and Maia Dalton-Theodore.

At the Johns Hopkins University, David Everett. At the University of Iowa: Connie Brothers, Deb West, Jan Zenisek. At Florida State: Carolyn Hector Hall, Tara Stamm, Debra Brock.

Mike Harvey, Mike Shupp, Damon Hennessy, Rob LeBourdais, Lisa Washburn, and most especially Glen Springer. The Kistulentz and Kendrick families. Tom and Valen Brown, Millie and Bill Kramer.

Eternal memory: Rebecca Schiek, Sandy Seay, Bob Dotolo, Adam Rutland, Chris M., Jewell Alexander, Randall Causley, Craig Arnold.

This book does not happen without Tracy. How I might repay you, I have no idea. I will try every day for the rest of my life.

Contents

The Luckless Age

The Luckless Age

I. World's Forgotten Twentieth-Century Boy

Here, my century as it actually was.

Complete with so many reasons not to tell what happened, morning in America
      again, shining city on a hill,
end of the Reagan era (*sic semper tyrannis*) and I was just twenty, doomed
to live in a shadowed minor landscape of glassined marble, where a confetti
      of love letters to Jodie Foster
floated down from the tinted windows of the lone gunman's favorite Hilton.
Season of breakups and flings, season of double gimlet and buffalo wing,
      insomniac soundtrack
provided by a cranky Frigidaire humming in Ringo Starr time.
Soundtrack of solemn barren apartment, liturgy with Gregorian chant
      of *She's in Parties*
or Lou Reed's apology, *I'm sorry that I did that/I'm sorry that I hit you,*
six months until the winter of my disconnection, insomnia unsoothed
      by midnight
applications of bourbon or the touch of blowsy, lipsticked strangers.

II. Places That Are Gone

Write the vision plain upon the tablets
—Habakkuk 2:2

That's the Old Testament, giving advice to heretical writers,
and for me, I take comfort in knowing how, centuries before
the appearance of this rumored Christ, poets were obsessed

with staying power, because what is the landscape
of a hometown but a growing laundry list of places
that are gone, Dart Drug and the Hot Shoppes Cafeteria

on Wisconsin Avenue, the dazed, meandering homeless
selling plastic roses liberated from the beaten-down
Moonie teenagers who pimped for the Unification Church?

Habakkuk got it wrong, though, I remember writing
in my notebook; the vision came clear with a disclaimer,
plain upon five- and ten-milligram EZ-gel caplets:

Do not operate heavy machinery. Side effects may include
ambient hallucinations ringing out like a warning
of the end of days, sandwichboard crazies who said

The end is nigh

because this was the Reagan era and the end *was* nigh,
those days of revelation—lower case "r"—where
what I learned in the wax-hot stillness of three a.m.

was nothing but a reaffirmation of what I already knew.
To have all those empty urges for richness and be lonely
is selfish, and I *was* selfish, have always been so, particularly

when jostled from the earliest sodden sleep
by a woman, bodice laced and head veiled, who bent
over the foot of my bed to whisper to me in a language

as foreign as Aramaic. What good can a visiting spirit
augur if I can never know what her tidings mean?
Has language ever been anything but an obstacle?

And the next night, I woke to a vision of Maglight-
wielding police flashing about my fourth-story balcony,
rousting a homeless man passed out on the fire escape,

moving him along with pointed jackboot. Still later,
in a series of end-of-the-world dreams, the moon
fell to the Earth in Texas-sized chunks, as if Saint John

had written a disaster film starring Bruce Willis.
What then must we do? meaning, what should we do
if we are certain in our knowledge: these are the end times?

Tolstoy couldn't answer the question, and Count Leo
was riffing on brother Luke, who could not answer it either.
Both asked, *What then must we do?* Meaning *I have tried*

nearly everything, as if they knew Monday's tepid pledges
of moderation would be abandoned in slow-cooked nightsweats,
that no desire was stronger than the desire to be adored

by strangers, except maybe the desire for a welcoming nod
from a heavy-pouring bartender. And there I was headed out
on the town, headlong into a luckless age of methamphetamine

and humbucking guitars, the feedback drone of Marshall amplifiers,
a bleeding cityscape of broken bottles and eleven-dollar martinis
at Chi-Cha Lounge; through a cityscape of storefront Salvadorans

drinking Modelo Especial and taunting the policewoman
with acrylic nails who spoke no Spanish; cityscape of the same
Salvadorans, ghost-dusted in sanded drywall compound,

choosing sides for Friday soccer, the war of shirts
versus skins delayed while daylaborers picked through
cityscape covered with used syringes on gravel-pocked field.

Cityscape of a high school too poor to field a football team
because it could not afford a safety fence—Hadrian's wall
in miniature—just as they could not provide security

on Friday evenings when off-duty cops stood like Beefeaters
outside the California Steak House, in front of a neon marquee
which lured me under with an arrow rimmed in amber light.

I might as well have slipped the cover charge under my tongue
instead of answering the siren call of three-chord juvenilia,
the engraved invitation of a bar sign that said, *This Is It!*

which it was.

Hotel Amsterdam

I'm holed up on 46th Street courtesy of the Amoco Travel club,
where a worldly Polish cabbie who fled to New York
two months before I did reminds me to fear the long night
of trouble I can find for forty dollars in the one white quarter
of the city too strung out to sleep.
                                    Instead I head out
to the tranny hookers and soul food joints of 9th Avenue,
following the movement of a Friday night where I walk
West across the river, or South towards the taxi garages
of Chelsea, where in staccato English, four cabdrivers
argue whether three of a kind beats two pair. I want to
pull up a folding chair at that poker table, complain
about the day's take and the medallion rent, and wait until
a bottle is produced and communion gained, to tell them
the rest:
            my feet are killing me, and my back; wait to ask
why English words get broken over our Slavic tongues.

And even before the dispatcher comes out of his cage
to tell me he has exactly what I want, I'll skip out, head
uptown to the safety of the Hotel Amsterdam, 10th floor,
past the desk clerk who finally asks if I need anything,
say more soap, for the night.
                              For an answer, there's a list

of what I need, starting with the camaraderie I've just seen,
just prayed to be invited into. Specific answers,
I mean. But I was twenty, and had no idea what I needed
except that since it was New York, and since I was twenty,
I knew it was out there, a certainty floating like a charge
across the grid of concrete and wire, all the possible troubles
that might come in amounts too much or too expensive,
all the calamities of a city where I was afraid to live.

Fixing

What I did
I did in the dark,
nightclub bathroom door
held shut by my bulk,
a twenty-dollar descent
into the uproar
of mad stupidity.
At least I used
a fresh needle,
and before I went
sick, drew the plunger
back, pressed it down
four times, filling
and emptying, and
filling again with blood.
I used a needle
only once, the night
before I married.
That ought to be enough
to convince anyone
in omens. Let's resist
moralizing here, just
say it was wrong,
meaning incorrect,

a subtle offense.
They call it fixing;
you do it because
you are broken;
and you hope
it will help,
and still later
you talk about it, this
one thing no one saw.

WILD GIFT

The world's a mess, it's in my kiss, said the song,
to which I said, play it louder, play it meaner.
Play it fast enough that your forearm muscles
burn and stand, Popeye-like, grotesque and proud.

And play it only for me, waiting stage right at the feet
of a bass player by the name of John Doe, anonymous
like us boys with our hair dyed chrome black, pegged
jean and leather jacketed boys so busy being homo-

genous even in our prayers, as each of us asked,
Let me be the only one, meaning the only one to whom
these words meant anything, the only one who played
it louder, meaner, the lead guitar in monophonic mix

squawking out the right channel of a blown speaker,
black noise from a season of amperes and high voltage,
high wattage electroencephalogram and anti-convulsive meds.
Season to pick up a pawnshop guitar and three chords,

learn how to love this dark world, the hours lost in it.
Season too when I learned how to talk to mothers
about sons lost to the dulcet sweep of heroin, learned
how forgetfulness can be purchased in twenty-dollar handfuls,

how to say with the inflections of a Swiss diplomat,
Your son will be often on his way but will seldom arrive.
I know now that no mother can ever be prepared to hear
the gossip of a junkie's death, all its ham-handed irony,

subtle as an afterschool special: I swear he only snorted,
he only chased the dragon. The first time a friend shot up,
under the pleasing and violent rain of his shower,
he nodded, fell, hitting his head on the soap dish,

bled to death on the ancient mosaic of his bathroom floor.
His girlfriend found his pruned and whitened body
when the water ran in the trickle of piss-streams downstairs
and the landlord poked a broom handle through

the sagging plaster ceiling until it fell in tectonic plates
to the floor. Or he shot up and drowned in the bath,
Morrison-esque; I cannot rightly remember, because
of my own weakness, because there were so many stories,

season of neglect, season of death. They call it fixing,
and you do it because you have been broken.
The nectar of the poppy is like holding a wolf
by the ears, and only those with ears shall hear

the siren call of *public service announcement with guitar*
the way me and my friend Bob did, lured unaware
onto the rocks. Why do broken boys pick up guitars?
An unanswerable riddle I am afraid, just as I am afraid

of the honest answer: none of us will ever be whole,
not even filled by the crescendo of *Won't Get Fooled Again*
which rose faster than the plume of blood in the plastic
tower of a ten-cc syringe with microfine needle,

blood in the chamber rising like an animated tornado,
the rush hitting, then quieting, as in the slow-breaking middle
eight of *Baba O'Riley* where another junkie guitarist implored
us not to cry, reminded us what we had learned firsthand:

at four a.m., it's only teenage wasteland. The city bleeds,
the city burns, deep into the heat season of crack and Len Bias,
season of self-etherization, season of *bitch set me up*.
Because I was one, a teenager, dancing like a spastic,

I learned how my ecstasies could never be anyone else's
ecstasies watching students from the college of the deaf
lean on the speakers as if practicing the laying on of hands,
dancing as a jukebox Vulcan mind meld. How I wanted

to dance like that, connected to music itself, which is why
whenever we could convince the women to dance,
we spread miles apart to the edges of the dance floor
then careened into each other, not like charged particles—

not even in the bruises of mosh pit chaos, because
even there a pattern emerges, indistinct at first—this
was more the chaos of bail bonds and car accidents,
four a.m. pancakes and the pettiest larcenies and going

home alone but together, the era of slamming doors
and broken plates, era of the dance floor between us,
era of the ocean in our bed. The radio told me, *Los Angeles
beckons teenagers to come to her on buses*, but I never left the city.

Heavy Metal Bob did, went to get clean in San Francisco,
junkie logic; no junk in that big a city, as if San Francisco
and its Tenderloin of plenty would ever be a place to go
quit anything. Bob died a couple years back, hanged himself.

The city bleeds and the wolf does not always bare his teeth
before he bites. I'm sorry to sum up the life of someone I loved
with this *American Graffiti*-type ending, but you knew how
life's wild gift comes to an end, because I'd already told you

when I said they call it fixing: we do it when we are broken.

THE BOURBON MYTHS

Today, I could not sit still for the needle,
having learned how the tattooing barb
never deposits the darkness, merely pulls out
the bitter parables already brewing beneath skin—
mine a watchful gargoyle on the left scapula,
a Pegasus ascending the opposite side.
Call them epaulets, artifacts from the time
when the graffiti of my body said all it could
of Gods and creation, when a needle chiseled
a pair of angels rising from meat and stone.

LUCKLESS AGE (SLIGHT RETURN)

After a glass of wine with the mother of God,
she moved off, away, towards the streets
filled with pine-scented taxis taking shortcuts
to an airport crowded with irregular pilgrims.
I stayed on, headed out on the town, headlong
back into that luckless age of no noise
reduction and opiated cough syrups.
I stayed on, waiting for my lungs
to clear out the cobweb sobs,
whatever it was that was suppressed.
I stayed on until night, the hollowest part
of that first empty day, waiting for midnight,
knowing how I loved our dark world,
our time together in it, how without reference,
something was wrong with the elements of air;
I was moving into a new season of no,
no drinking or children, no God or peace.

Roaratorio

for Frank Conroy (d. April 6, 2005)

At that level of vodka where night becomes magnanimous,
let us be true primitives and swing to a quiet species
of jazzology, that deductive science so intuitive at four a.m.
That's the hour when everything—birds, leaves, clouds—
has an order unto itself, and two fish spring about
like young dogs. Only an imbecile tries to kiss time,
or demands sense of all the music, the smoky meannesses,
while his stomach rebels, eyes spinning in the green rings
of a turntable, ergo that's gotta be Philly Joe Jones
beating it out, then Oscar Peterson, playing blue notes
with verve, a tympani of fingers half tiger, half felt.

Elegy for the Bay City Rollers

This was the era of fat, drunk Truman Capote,
      sucking midnight highballs at 54, wondering

why everyone stared at Bianca, Paloma or Liz, never seeing
      the allure in such a continental parade of breast.

A band landed at Kennedy; even Murray the K came back
      for the moment's resurrection of live television,

spewing first-day rumors of screaming girls, each greased
      a ten-spot by coke-hoarding record company execs.

Retail stores closed at five, thermostats frozen at sixty-eight,
      we held hands that winter only in the practical search

for radiant warmth; we were all clamoring for heat.
      Then the Rollers kicked in the door to *American Top 40*,

and we raised the antennae of our disappointment
      one last time, to hear a bottle-blonde and -weary singer

stretching lyrics over a framework of threadbare arrangements.
      "I" became a quatrain, meaning we just couldn't wait

a full measure of patience. But the song was a retread, stolen,
     like most good things in rock and roll, from two black guys.

The planets in alignment, *Merry Christmas, war was over,*
     Skylab showered us with the spit of magnesium

fire falling across oceans and continents. Ed Sullivan was dead
     and so was the mania, The Beatles just four musicians,

solo artists longer than they had been a group.
     The time for hope had been wasted,

between Dallas and Memphis and the Ambassador Hotel.
     It was damn cold, and the liberty of gasoline so dear.

The President's malaise seeped in, gas from the vents,
     soaking us, and we hoped it could burn off

in the fireglow aftermath of one last explosion. Instead,
     we got the Rollers, their two-and-a-half minute pop gems

flickering out a transient sputter of red and green, Fourth
     of July sparklers, incandescent, hot only for the moment.

THE SINATRA VILLANELLE

Want to know what was said in that vinyl restaurant booth?
Think Sinatra crying highballs when Ava hightailed it for good,
the mournful croon of *I took each word she said as gospel truth*.

Order a drink from old Toots: double gin, a splash of vermouth;
light a Pall Mall, eavesdrop from where Gleason stood,
the jukebox whispering what she said in that saloon booth.

She ran off with a teenaged matador, and his bright embroidered suit
hangs on Frank's old oaken hangar, above his polished boots.
That's what you get when you take what she says as gospel truth.

I took out a woman about to leave, dinner as an anniversary truce,
and consoled myself with Manhattans, light on the sweet vermouth,
the night she pronounced our death in a cavernous restaurant booth.

History means mistakes, poking like a child at a loosened tooth,
two stubborn actors rubbing six-dollar bourbon into their wounds,
all because they mistook the simplest words we say as gospel truth.

It's last call, but don't go yet. Be a stand-up guy like Frank or Toots.
The broad leaves, a pal stays, that's the song. Send a drink if you would,
Listen to Frank tell how the story ends, alone in that booth.
I'd always known she'd turn me down. That's the gospel truth.

. . . BUT THE LITTLE GIRLS UNDERSTAND

for Doug Fieger (d. 2010), Berton Averre, Prescott Niles and
Bruce Gary (d. 2006)

The men don't know growls
Willie Dixon's most famous tune, but
the version I prefer—low fidelity
cassette bootleg, howling tin sound with
shredded paper drums—remains
unreleased, recorded not by some venerable
Mississippi blues curmudgeon
whose name, artfully dropped here,
would evoke afternoons porch-sitting
with magnolia wine and box-string guitar,
or might bestow upon me
some sorely lacking hipster bonafides.
That's never going to happen,
since I am talking here
about a nearly unlistenable cover,
the monophonic noise and mid-range screech
of The Knack, live in Hollywood,
before a packed house at the Troubador,
July 1979. So what if I was twelve?
I'd already gotten it, learned how to pluck
out the gallop of *My Sharona*'s bass,
hoping someday I'd ace out Doug Fieger
and be Sharona's back door man

myself, though I'd have been better off
learning how to get in the front door first.
Which was the vaguest country,
women, or the blues? I did not know.
I still might not. I only knew
what I was learning: that a song
could actually sound like sweat;
that Ray Manzarek, gangly Ray best known
as the piano-playing witness to greatness,
had dropped by to sit in,
and when he'd come down Wonderland Avenue
it was a benediction, as if to say, *Hey,
these guys are all right,* forgive them
their sins of leather tie and Beatle boot.
So I want to say thank you
to whoever thought to tape that show,
because it taught me that I wanted a forever
girl like Sharona, who,
as the 45-rpm picture sleeve promised,
played the coolest records
for her slumber-partying girlfriends,
who all looked like the camisoled girls
in the Runaways or the equally fated Go-Gos.
But I am getting ahead of myself, since,

as Leonard Cohen says, everybody knows
how this story ends. I have everything
The Knack ever recorded, including
this version of *Back Door Man*,
which tells me everything that was wrong
with 1979, and later, everything wrong with me.
How does the show end? Listen
to the cassette, a moment in unsteady time,
the Zapruder film of the skinny tie era.
For the band, you know how it ends
already: rehab, divorce, rehab, forgiveness,
comeback tour, state fair nostalgia;
immortal Sharona—her real name
—sells real estate, million-dollar homes.
That's what those little girls do,
they grow up, which reminds me
My Sharona, that set-closing number,
may be the saddest story I know.

THE PICTURE OF HANK WILLIAMS, SR., TAKEN BY MY GRANDFATHER IN GERMANY

That's what we fought over the last time—
drunk like Hank, I clogged your driveway
with a ton of muddy pickup
and two hundred twenty pounds of me.
Okay, two forty. That's not the point.
The plan was to steal the picture back,
tack it over my desk, unframed,
because Hank was a simple man,
direct as a left jab,
all whiskey and beer, and one, four, five
in the key of G.
In the picture, there's a woman
or a girl, dressed up.
Hank's in a suit, too.
She might be inspiration,
a backup singer we didn't recognize,
servicing Hank on the bus.
It had to be love, or something like it,
since the agnostic in you
would not consider a man
taking his hat and his guitar
to Deutschland just for the beer.
So, now you know why I'm here,
conniving my way back home,

because the picture of Hank Williams, Sr.,
taken by my grandfather in Germany
should never be under glass,
unless it's a tumbler,
three sweet fingers of bourbon on ice.

The Rick Springfield Sonnet

Jessie's girl hears her song, *Top 40 Countdown*,
then calls Rick to complain, *How could you?*
which pleases him, leaves him soap opera smug.
The master plan is probably moot; it's just Rick,
afflicted with love, like so many other guitarists
of the feathered hair, Members Only jacket
type, and someone's already beaten him
to writing a song called *My Best Friend's Girl*.

I like to think Jessie's girl is named Sarah,
Hebrew for *princess*, because Jessie means
God sees, and surely everyone else can see
what Rick is up to, his charade of cool lines.
That doesn't mean the plan isn't a brilliant,
seductive sleight of hand. Rick knows, Rick waits.

THE END OF THE AFFAIR AS FORETOLD IN LANGUAGE FROM THE REVELATION OF SAINT JOHN THE DIVINE

This summer everything felt retro,
       even the Bee Gees were happening again,

and I wasted the whole time thinking—
       about the tortures of sweetness—and of you,

dreamy in the slow and drunk-eyed way
       men who never came all the way back

sputtered on about Vietnam, first wives.

We were a series of omens: the first one,
       a phrenology of clotted tea leaves

at the bottom of a yellow porcelain mug,
       predicted us—I saw the vision—

so I made the mistake of history,
       I *assumed* something, and you know

what the pop etymology of that word
       suggests about *assuming*.

So we happened, inevitable as
      Romulus counting birds.

My own predictions were for
      your naked form in my bed,

but the only thing of yours I touched
      was pity, the same generic pause

you'd give to those blank men, homeless
      or desperate. What else can I say

about three foul months where suddenly
      you, with your plastic tiger doll eyes,

were a little Miss Nostradamus,
      with predictions of our doom?

Your words were a different seductress,
      and at least with the liquor I always had

some idea of the grandeur of my demise,
      since I had visited it a few times before.

The heart is a foolish muscle, and I suffered
    the migrainous visions of nightmares,

where whole eggs lodged in the soft pouch
    of my swelling Dizzy Gillespie cheek,

the skin of the shell breaking under the strain,
    crushing my teeth; fragments, crowns,

shards of porcelain, and an albumen drool
    curdled over my lips, and I could not speak,

except to shout the irrational,
    but because I was lukewarm—
    neither cold nor hot—

you finally spat me out.

THE EVEL KNIEVEL FUCK POEM

The crowd's gasping inhalations are the sharpest death rattle
echoing across my desert continent. I never linger over beauty,
until a thing has at least once been shattered, then stitched together,
and I know you, too, must feel this way, as your fingers dawdle
over the story of every canyonesque scar on this blessed, broken body.

Let me take you on a tour of the man-made wonders of the world,
the Boulevard Saint Germain at Kings Island,
the colossus of the Astrodome, the oompah music and beer halls
of Busch Gardens, the carnivals of every state fair
midway, butter cows and fried Twinkies, cotton candy and pan drippings.

Come let me wash your hair in the mineral-rich waters
of the Caesar's Palace fountains, and only after I lick
the corn-dog grease from your death-thin fingers will I tend to your tresses
with brushes made of badger hair and combs of black-market ivory.
After this counterfeit wedding, the crowds will chant our names in concert,

and cheer as they do whenever I emerge unscathed. We will wave
from the top of the ramp in the manner of dictators
while the hordes shout their demands to see sullied bed sheets,
which, because I am a showman, I shall affix 'round your neck,
as I would bestow a cape on a loyal sidekick. The forces that compel crowds

to gather mean we all wish to witness the spectacle of violent death,
and the sound of an engine—the v-twin high-octane moan—
is regret, a chorus of voices saying goodbye to something that never was.
You will tell the assembled masses of your wildest wish to fly,
this most solemn promise witnessed by Jim McKay of *Wide World of Sports,*

and only because you never asked the obvious question of why
it is that I do what I do, I will endeavor a serious answer:
Never for God or mammon. For every thrill of victory, there is the agony
concomitant with defeat. I arrive at night because I am a messenger
of end times, jumping over carcasses, flying over civilization's marrow bones.

Hot Child in the City

Never once after Iggy Pop told me, *Young girls, they know what they're after,*
did I think of Roanoke, Virginia, since after all, what Iggy was saying
was just another way to remind us how
Los Angeles beckons the teenagers to come to her on buses,
a line I've lifted from another song, but the point is this:
Kundera might have called it eternal return,
the girls arriving as naïve pilgrims from Abilene, Ypsilanti, Youngstown, Ohio.

Because that's what the image becomes, *Youngs*-town,
in a city of screeds and ultimatums. VHS cassettes of *Naughty Newcummers*
(Volume 42) play as white noise in the background.
They come to Youngstown and leave as nothing more than spent fuel rods,
burning and dangerous for the rest of a half-life.
This happened to a girl I knew,
the muffled shouting moans of porn like background music

as Becky talked to her mother, dialing 1-800 COLLECT, Becky high
at four a.m., white knuckling her way to another tequila sunrise.
So young indeed, but surely old enough to know better
than to trust California and its vicious lessons of reinvention.
If Los Angeles could speak, it would say only, *Goodbye, Norma Jean,*
before letting out a tremendous belch.
And after the great quake, the Irwin Allen disastrousness

predicted by no less an authority than Steely Dan, California would
actually tumble into the sea, the result of writhing tectonic plates,
                   and, if there is such a thing as justice, find itself
reincarnated as Roanoke, the Hollywood sign a gaseous apparition
                        over the very same thirty-dollar Shenandoah Valley motel
where Becky begged her mother to fetch her,
              to permit her safe retreat to the familiar womb of a basement

        with a working washer-dryer, Sunday dinner after mass at St. Bernadette's.
The real ending to Becky's story would never sit well with a screening audience.
              Too dark, they'd say, craving the spun-sugar confection
of another rehab romance, but this is a disaster movie, ending in room 27
of the Carillon Motor Court, Becky hanging up the phone,
                   then pouring two gallons of gasoline over her body.
She'd gone to Los Angeles, and met a man who introduced her to confections

        of his own—Quaaludes and cocaine and ten-milligram Xanax.
She should have known the invitation, *Come on down to my place, baby,*
              meant every fairy tale can also be a tragedy;
Cinderella's stepsisters cut off their toes trying to pack their feet, sausage-like,
        into someone else's slipper. Becky's mother said only sleep it off,
                   she'd have a clearer view of things in the morning.
But this is a genre story, without the possibility of a prince or a happy end,

        just a match, then fire, a girl who thought she needed a big bad wolf.

O My Badlands: A Soundtrack

Stark weather rolling across the badlands,
      rocking-chaired between heavy metal kiddies—
trippers and askers—prancing through wheatgrass,
      their spindly legs arrayed in rayon, spandex.

Three-chord monty, the *Back in Black* overture,
      an AM station sparkles then fades at dusk,
chicken-fried steak in a gas station diner,
      The Hawkeyes moving left to right across your dial.

April's end means an Interstate 40 love song, *boom,*
      boom, out go the lights in a slow motion whirl
across the concrete highways of the Panhandle,
      rancid winter lingering like the smell of fish.

The velvet fog drenching southern Illinois,
      low rider, exit ramps without safety railings,
an overloaded truck listing to starboard,
      the forecast: bluster and thunder across the plains.

Losing my religion? Ridgefield, Utah.
      Implied narratives about muscle-y girls
and teenaged cars. Dairy Queen voyeurs
      peep at cheerleaders rimming sugar cones.

Poor man wanna be rich, rich man wanna be king.
Jersey mythos, as vast as empires.
When someone says he contains multitudes,
   what he means is: *I'm bad, I'm nationwide.*

Fuck Poem with Language Borrowed from the Gospel According to Saint Mark

As it is written, a list of things we did not, and shall never do:
such as go elsewhere, into the next town where we were unknown
yet still beautiful as if I had not been sick with this lunatic fever
that I have had since you moved here.
                                        In the next town
we did not take a meager room behind the stables. The radio never spoke
the false promise of voluptuous days, and I did not fill the bedside
table's only drawer with Swedish sex toys and stolen bottles
of booze or offer you wine mixed with gall.
                                        Your body never dripped
with wild honey and come, and you did not gird yourself
to the headboard with leather straps or blindfold me with silks.

I did not invade the Sudetenland of tan lines and razors,
and when you did not emerge naked and unshy from the lake,
your body did not appear to the astigmatic me as a tree,
or any other beautiful thing.
                                        Number me among the rheumatoid
and the infirm of heart. The next time you allow your fingers
to graze the hillocks of your own hip, the whole lovely parade,
you will learn why I speak in blasphemies. I need to put my fingers in
your wounds to believe, which is why I went to the lake's edge
alone, and asked no one to follow. Instead, I spent night and day
crying out and bruising myself with slick, moss-covered stones.

BARGAIN

The songs that summer spoke only
in the imperative voice, *jump, shout, relax,*
even though everyone knew what a bad idea
it was to demand anything of teenagers.
Besides, we wanted testimony, witness,
to suffer the insufferable and survive;
for my sins, that's exactly
what I got. So when I said, *I'd pay
any price just to win you,* I meant Southern
Comfort and ginger, gutwater and iodine,
and twenty years of knowing how sad it is
to be aphastic, another sodden minstrel
speaking of remembered joys,
a naked body I will never again
touch. I preferred more honest bargains,
the quid pro quos of townhouse basements or
Plymouth backseats or even the 1971 Volkswagen Beetle
I remember with one brown door.
Someday I might want to be a secret again,
kept from someone's mother, and not
the pleasant neighborly boy
she remembers, filed away in the category
of *whatever happened to,* island
of lost luggage. But suppose

we woke up and it was 1985 again;
how would we recognize the death-thin
finger of fate tapping us
on the shoulder unless it pushed
us down into the same
two back-of-the-bus seats
with their pockmarked burns that smelled
of dry mustard? A secret is
only a secret if it is never told
and this one is nothing
but the memory of negotiations, incidents
and accidents and yes, hints
and allegations, too.
The ghost in you haunts
the theater at the Springfield Mall;
we will never again be as close
as the passenger seat, on those mornings
when—*brain fried day-glo*—
we refused to say good night. Ambiguity,
you said, is best washed away with
five-dollar champagne. We would be lovers
until the missiles were flying, hallelujah,
a promise made before God and Mary
Jane Clement in second period Latin,

unsanctified, useless, forever unfulfilled.
Reagan went to Reykjavik, and we went
to a mythical place called *college*,
where I cannot recall a single thing we did,
except to know I have not, until now,
felt as close to the end
of the world.

You Don't Love Me (You Don't Care)

I have never been permitted to return
to a specific year, the one I would choose
if time travel were a reward, something to redeem
for a million frequent flyer miles. Disruptions
in the space-time continuum aside, all of us would
return to that place of first permission, wouldn't we?
I would, to the aforementioned Volkswagen,
seats covered in the crumbs of shoplifted doughnuts,
to Christmas morning gifts—silk knot cufflinks,
awash in the bottom of a porcelain beer mug
painted with the logo of the defunct haberdasher
where I once bought a tie for Ted Bundy,
(true story)—but that's another poem entirely.
So what is this? A benediction, a dismissal, a letter
on another occasion, and how sad it is to see this
become a laundry list of things I'd like to do (again)
but cannot. Too much has been said about the binds
of time, and the ties that bind, and baby, our love
went on for days. The radio gave us messages
and you were the Tokyo Rose of punk rock.
How soon is now? The truth hits everybody,
all the best cowboys etc., *Every Breath You Take*
is a song about stalking that people insist on playing
at weddings. You should never need to have love

explained, least not in my clumsy unrhymed ways—
think of it as porn, familiar when it plays.
I carved your name in oak, a bar top rune.
Our song was just a song and I can name that tune
in three notes. *A love that's love*, to a Bo Diddley beat,
d.c. al coda, which means lather, rinse, repeat.

Fuck Poem with Language Borrowed from Brothers Karamazov

Perhaps only the happy dead of winter can slow the creeping mold
            on the loaf of brown bread your mother handed over.
The ultimate consolation prize, meaning you will leave, but I should not starve.
                   In the same breath, a priest would tell you:
This is my body, broken for you, he might offer a more common prayer,
              avoid every kind of falsehood, especially to yourself.
       Fill in your own jokes about whiskey and confession here,
but never mention how I asked for a dirtier secret, which I then gleefully retold.

                     When I asked you to shock me, I meant
         tell me about the incandescent moments before you come,
not something as pedestrian as the tale of your first lover, now dead.
       Soon it will be spring and we can return to being the pagans
we have always wanted to be,
        and I can be convicted of nearly half of what I've actually done.

     Active love is labor and fortitude, but to be a villain you must learn
how the constant black hat is a tiresome pose, and never pretend
                  that it is backbreaking work.
         I'm sorry I can say nothing more consoling to you,
except come back to our bed so we can give people the harsh, dreadful thing
       they so desire, since everyone sees themselves in a tragedy,
               especially one with a happy end.

The David Lee Roth Fuck Poem with Language Taken from *Van Halen I, 1984,* and the First Letter of the Apostle Paul to the Church at Corinth

What you are expecting is a familiar riff on the theme
of girls and cars, where Laurel Canyon rings with big beast reverb
and in the top-down weather, the freeways clog with dinosaur
machines all pointed towards the water gone green,
sky lighting up the boulevard, Pacific Ocean blue poured on gasoline.

It's a new leather jacket and stiletto boots and four girls
from high school, too young but still cute, pink high tops and hula hoops
in the back of Daddy's Cadillac, 455 cubic inches of open throat,
the sound a boy makes when he imitates *hot shoes*
burning down the avenue. I pass and I leer and they give me

the universal salute, extended middle finger, even the driver,
both hands off the wheel. We orbit the light, circle the block and I tell them
the most honest thing I know: *The way of love is the highway,*
and in your malice you are still children. I was sent to give
sparkling advice in strange tongues, though my tongue should cease,

because all you have to do is slide down out of the hillsides
and see the runaways staggering up Sepulveda, begging quarters for the RTD.
Hollywood is the gaping maw of an insatiable clown that devours
everything it sees, indiscriminate in its appetites, and soon
you girls will be dancing seven sets a night, three songs a set,

garbed in the sacramental costumes of sexy librarians
or Catholic school nurses, whatever. We *ain't talking 'bout love,*
but rather the feel of velvet creamy dollars tucked into a saggy garter,
the soundtrack reminders to take care of your bartender,
your waitress, for every dancer down to just her fishnets to Windex

mirror and pole at the end of each three-song set, house rules,
and be sure to tip out the busboys who so deliriously vow to become men
who drive convertibles with white vinyl interiors and festoon
the rearview with dice and a piña colada-scented freshener.
It is as if California causes blindness, an inability to see the future.

So let me tell you how it is going to be: once the evening
is gas-filled for ten dollars a tank, everybody who wants some can park
at Carl's Junior and walk to curbside, where a pony-tailed girl
waits only for someone willing to listen to the tribulations
of being 14, to sing her a love song of how the six-dollar burger

once only cost three, and hope alternately meant the sound
of Stratocasters or glass-pack mufflers, or even the big beat of bass drum,
and if I speak in the tongues of men I am only a clanging cymbal
of warnings, part known, part obvious. There's always
a Doctor Feelgood paying off cops in the back of Winchell's Donuts,

and there's always a guy waiting out back with a business card,
one that says *producer*, but who actually owns the Carl's Junior franchise
down the block, and he says things like: Come run away with me,
because that is what a girl must learn to do when she casts aside
her Topeka past. Come run away with me for a six-dollar burger

laden with any condiment you desire. And me, Diamond Dave,
I am a messenger here with this fair warning. That man, what he desires
is to reach down between his legs and ease the seat back, and he'll tell you
to leave the shoes on. Stand firm. Let nothing move you.
I'll tell him myself: *Don't you know she's coming home with me?*

Wonderamaland

As a child my greatest dream—surpassing even my first-grade desire
to teleport myself from the chaos of Miss Jane Northcutt's classroom
        back to the swaddled coziness of bed and a threadbare stuffed dog—

        was to be a victim, to take a pie in the face from Soupy Sales,
suffer a compound fracture of the fibula, all for the misdemeanor of helping
        Wile E. Coyote assemble one Acme product or another.

                                                I'd get batted upside

        the head with a cast-iron skillet, then shake away the cobwebs
and bluebirds of concussed dreams and enter at last into the kingdom
        promised us,
where Monty Hall and I made a deal for whatever

        was found behind door number 3, and a showgirl parted the curtain
while Johnny Olson told me what I'd won: a tweedy Barcalounger, say,
one that turned into Captain Video's ejection seat.
                                                I'd pull the handle

        to launch myself into a nearly blank animated landscape
where my best friend was a talking dog—a purple Airedale terrier
        who wore a monocle and waistcoat, and spoke in a clipped British

upper-class lockjaw—who of course spoke only to me,
as in the compound shenanigans of Mister Ed or that Warner Brothers frog
who bojangled in top hat and tails.
Or I'd just step into the swimming

mercury of the picture tube, move into the third hut on the left
and share the last slice of Gilligan's coconut cream pie, or I'd be the anonymous hipster
playing a passable sax for the mambo kings of Ricky Ricardo.

And after the two-drink minimum of the midnight show, I'd take
the long way home, and because I was hours late for supper, a voice with all
the stentorian authority of Morrow reporting from London would echo

across the five boroughs, asking, *It's ten o'clock, do you know
where your children are?* And I would answer in my best call and response, a shout:
I am meandering through a veritable Wonderamaland filled with neighbors

who still bake pies and, once a week, pay the neighbor's kid six bits
to wash their car. On Saturday nights, Mom and Dad rhumba away
the evening at a Knights of Columbus dinner dance for twenty bucks

a couple, beer and set-ups provided. Friday, Dad gets a haircut—
one dollar, military or civilian—then drives home in a new white Mercury,
window down and the crackling ga-lump of the *Ballantine Polka Hour*

hissing out the AM radio, followed by Paul Harvey telling *the rest of the story.* The neighbors gather for hot dogs and beer and to touch the car's pearlescent enameled shroud and kick its white sidewall tires

then head home at seven p.m. to watch Roger Mudd sitting in for Walter Cronkite, who isn't on assignment but sailing off the Vineyard, and the top stories are all entirely forgettable.

Vietnam is a word no one knows,

the children of Cam Le play with dolls instead of a GI's Zippo. Edmund Muskie never gets ratfucked and doesn't cry in the snows of New Hampshire, and when the whole world is watching,

Bobby Kennedy goes on to Chicago and wins there. And when I tell this or any story of my own childhood, I begin with the absolute truth. Such as in the ritualistic farce known as show and tell, when I show

my kindergarten classmates how to make daiquiris by the blenderful, and in the telling, wave my arms over my head and have them chant along with me the first words I ever spoke:

Look at all these fabulous prizes.

Pavarotti on Television

Midnight Christmas Eve, here's Luciano—
stuffed in white tie and tails, all hints of gray
dyed out of his wispy Abe Lincoln beard—
croaking and belting *Adeste Fidelis*;
it's the Saturday before the Lord's birth
and my mother-in-law is dying,
my family has fled to Arkansas.
This year, change has not been for the good.
Even Luciano looks sick, or old,
maybe both, his starched waistcoat too big
even for him. Tomorrow, I'll stuff two pounds
of lobster inside a six-pound tenderloin,
go through another pound or two
of butter making sauces and sweets.
I'll have help, but the table is for eight,
and making the grocery lists, I'll realize
this Christmas means a shortage of time,
no one to buy thoughtful gifts, no one singing
even the most ordinary hymns of praise.

Playing the Lead

For the exit scene, in the movie of my life,
I wanted to depend on the authority
of an actor's voice to give my excuses
some moral weight. Mastroianni understood
how to do this. He would know, with no coaching,
how to make the hard things I would have to say
to get out of the house sound mature, serious;
he could give my proclamations gravitas.
With another actor, the cadence
would be way off, he would never smoke
the right way; some soap-opera cavalier
might just toss my blue raincoat aside.

Marcello would know to turn down the stereo
for once, but never to put down the coat,
and never to discuss failure in the bedroom.
He'd leave the raincoat over his left shoulder;
cigarette in teeth, he'd fumble for matches
and look at his scuffed, yet expensive loafers,
telling my wife how what goes wrong between people
can sometimes be made right with some great labor.
But he'd be ready to leave far earlier;
he'd show her his smooth hands, fingers stained yellow,
explaining they were never meant for hard work.

THE SKIPPER TALKS TO HIS THERAPIST

for Alan Hale, Jr. (d. 1990)

Finally I've thrown away the hat, the way
      you suggested, but I can still smell it,
the candied aftermath of coconut oil,
      cocoa butter, all those salves and lotions
we made for ourselves. And it still
      makes me hungry, famished really.
I'm an overeater, okay, seeking comfort
      in the radiant heat of steam tables,
buffets, all-you-can-eat luncheons;
      my new passion is the super-size.
Desire has always meant a T-bone,
      which, come to think, is a word that sounds hot,
sexy, something two guys in the Village
      might be doing at a Turkish bath. I never miss
a meal, but I've cried once or twice
      when I realize how I miss the connection
between men, in all their different types,
      sailors and stockbrokers and eggheads.

By the time I'd been on that island
      a year, I'd wasted maybe three months
of it beating off to torn magazine pages
      of an unattainable beauty, a redhead
who was fading before my eyes, going soft
      like the bananas I ate every damn day.

Even someone who did not go far
        in school knows paradise has its downfall;
Isn't that the great lesson of history?
        Then there you are, under stalks
of bananas, everything turning brown
        under noonday sun, waiting for girls
half your age and one-third your weight
        to sidle over the stovetop sand, hoping
for a tolerable glimpse of shoulder, or neck,
        or the white top of her ass, some vision
for the long night of manual pleasures.
        But what you really miss are the men.

I've been thinking about what you said
        last week, and I guess you're right,
we have had a breakthrough. The smells
        brought me back, the bay rum
and the precision of lime following
        a six o'clock shave, four survivors crowding
around a triangle of polished aluminum,
        searching in their faces for any hint
of why being this close to men
        feels the way that it does, why we build
these rituals just to touch each other's skin.

Changeling

for Dick York (d. 1992)

The end starts with Dick York's last recurring dream: his teeth crumbling into a curdled mess, bathing his tongue with a powder the consistency of laundry soap. A disappointing image, the books tell him, a *woman's* dream. Later today he's got to kiss Lizzie, has to be convincing as her lover. That's never been too difficult—on Monday nights, half the nation thinks of kissing the bewitching Samantha Stephens. But Lizzie Montgomery won't want to kiss toothless Dick, even though they play long-suffering husband and sultry wife; Lizzie and her slim capri pants, Lizzie's complex scent floating like incense out of the pink sweaters she wears around the set, her custom-blended perfume a gift from the producers at one hundred dollars a half-ounce. Lizzie's smell, with its hints of vermillion, still *incites*, even at a distance of thirty years. Lizzie, who sometimes read his cues from offstage, her hair in a towel; Lizzie, who thought it was cute how Dick York sometimes got hard as they choreographed scenes in their tiny kitchen; Lizzie, the first woman he'd ever known to wear a red bra.

But it was never his teeth, it was his back, killing him. They worked around it for five years, Darrin Stephens always sitting at his desk, on the couch, collapsing into a Barcalounger like the one Dick York sleeps in at home, thirty years on, still dreaming of Lizzie. But how will he kiss her with no teeth? Near the end, he's hooked up to an oxygen tank hidden behind his recliner, and still can't get a breath, can't do this final interview without the breathing tube taped to his upper lip. He can only manage to tell a reporter his version of the story—he quit the show because of his back. Dick York couldn't go on with the strain of series television, and Lizzie couldn't wrinkle her nose to make things any better. In his final days, Dick never mentions the money he lost, the show of his own, *Dick York, Dick York*, that lasted exactly seven weeks, the friends who sued. He wasn't jealous—Lizzie made them a mint. But sometimes he found himself staring at Lizzie the way field horses surround an uppity yearling, nuzzling, nipping at its withers with sharp, piano key teeth. Other times he found himself so angry he feared his red color might show through the lights and filters, and the audience might learn how much effort it took for Dick York to hold it all in, until he shook with the strain, until, without the trick lighting, without the grand mal madness from the pain pills and B12 shots, he began to change before their eyes—so subtly, something no one remarked on, a subject avoided in polite company, until the very end, when Dick York looked almost entirely like someone else.

Abyssinia

for McLean Stevenson (d. 1996)

Abyssinia: interjection, slang. Mid 20th century. I'll be seeing you (said on parting).
—*The Oxford English Dictionary*

Winter's nostalgia wave drags the man who played Colonel Blake
back to the talk show circuit. Hawkeye and Hot Lips sit on Carson's plaid couch,
    guffaw with Ed McMahon and ask, "Hey, Johnny, how about that drink?,"
but McLean Stevenson does phone interviews in his bathrobe, AM radio.
    He's an afterthought, selling term-life insurance on television.

    A week before they film the final episode, a Santa Ana brushfire
roars out past Studio City, turning the Army surplus of the *M*A*S*H* set to cinders.
    Ashes to ashes, junk to junk,
                the firefighting helicopters pull away
in odd numbers, plagues of locusts or fleeing birds. And whatever the reason,
    I remember January 1983 this way:
                    sixteen, immortal in the way
        only teenagers and crackheads can be, I stood on the 28th-floor
balcony of a Times Square hotel, conducting experiments in aerodynamics and flight,
        bombarding the courtyard with a fusillade of empty bottles. The percussion
of police baton on hotel door rang with the urgency of Charlie Watts,
    one, two, three, pausing,
              like Charlie, always on the four.
    Telling this story to an old friend, her main question stayed unspoken.
But it was the same question I'd always wanted to ask McLean Stevenson:

Suppose you could stand again at the very moment you knew in retrospect
as shot through with bad judgment, like the moment he quit the show?
    But no one ever asked.
                        No one asked either why the rutted and blood-soaked
            hills of South Korea bore a passing likeness to California,
one more congruence the couch-bound never noticed, the way Dick York morphed
        into Dick Sargent.
                    From the rubble of that hotel courtyard,
    I expected someone might ask about my drinking, if only for the same curious reasons
        people still ask about Yankee centerfielders. But why does anyone ask
            about DiMaggio unless the question has already been answered;
    Mister Coffee stutters across our memory only in the Ballantine Ale-nostalgia
        of sped-up 8-millimeter highlights.
                            So whenever someone asks
    about those bottles crashing to the sidewalk, I tell them the glint from the broken glass
        of cheap champagne is as exquisite as any stained mosaic
            of Saint John the Divine and his beatific face, counting lambs, books
    and seals. Or I tell them I don't know why I did it, the answer I suppose
        McLean gave from time to time. Why leave the trappings of stardom,
    make an inexplicable choice?
                        He could be proud—salt of middle American earth,
            sage uncle of Bloomington, Illinois—for the one piece of solid advice
                he gave us, as if he were our father: *Rule number one in war
    is that sometimes young men die, and rule number two is that sometimes doctors*

cannot change rule number one.
Worthy advice for our own times,
even for his own departure, when Radar O'Reilly stumbled in, murmuring,
Lieutenant Colonel Henry Blake's plane was shot down over the Sea of Japan,
and we wished Henry Godspeed, goodbye, farewell, amen.

About the Poet

Steve Kistulentz's poetry has appeared in numerous literary magazines, including the *Antioch Review*, the *Black Warrior Review*, the *Crab Orchard Review*, the *New England Review*, *Caesura*, *New Letters*, and *Quarterly West*. His work was selected for inclusion in the *Best New Poets* anthology by former Poet Laureate of the United States Mark Strand, and also appeared in the *Helen Burns Anthology: New Voices from the Academy of American Poets*. He is a two-time winner of the Academy's John Mackay Shaw Prize. He holds graduate degrees from the Johns Hopkins University, The University of Iowa Writers' Workshop, and the Florida State University. He was born and raised in the Washington, DC, area, and now teaches creative writing and literature at Millsaps College in Jackson, Mississippi, where he lives with his wife and daugher.